Foreword

Welc... ...raft book... ...Reny!" This is my 4th book and I am very excited to share new ideas with you. Adventure awaits!

Join me in visiting the fabulous zoo and the various exotic animals we will craft together. The book is divided into three sections: small, medium, and large animals.

I'm combining my years of experience as a kindergarten teacher, and over 1000 crafts that I've shared online, to convince you that crafting is easy and fun to do!

When you finish this book, you will have a great collection of amazing animal crafts to enjoy with your children or class. Enjoy!

Who's Reny?

I'm a kindergarten teacher and have been a craft blogger since 2015 making paper craft videos and tutorials.

I'm followed by millions of teachers and parents just like yourself from all around the globe.

Email me for free coloring templates!

Everyone loves freebies, right? :) I have prepared 40 coloring templates for you from my first book in one PDF file, ready for printing.

You can use them at home or make copies for your class or any activities with children.

Just email me and I will send you a copy with my sincere thanks for getting this book :)

My email is:

craftingwithreny@gmail.com

Tips & Tricks

Here are quick instructions to make funny eyes.

The next pages will cover shapes and dimensions for all the crafts in the book.

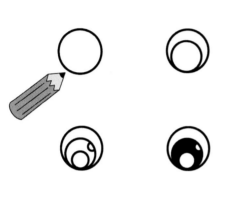

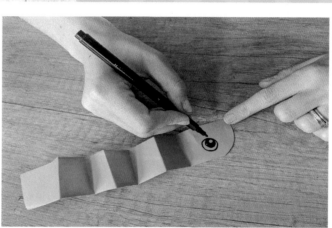

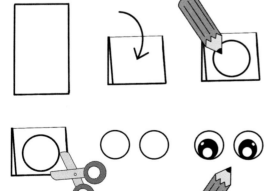

Tips for making circles and squares

A4

210 × 297 mm

Any sheet thickness

Or

Letter

8.5 × 11 in

Any sheet thickness

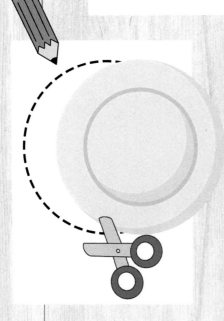

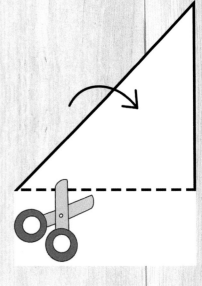

200 × 200 mm

8 × 8 inch

65 × 65 mm

2.5 × 2.5 inch

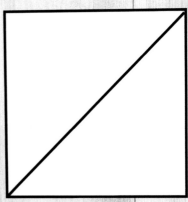

210 × 210 mm

8.5 × 8.5 inch

Tips for making strips

A4

210 × 297 mm

Any sheet
thickness

or

Letter

8.5 × 11 in

Any sheet
thickness

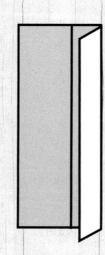
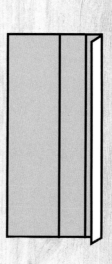

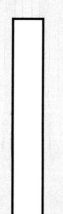
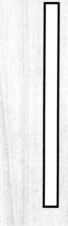

**1/2 of
A4 or Letter**

**1/4 of
A4 or Letter**

**1/8 of
A4 or Letter**

SMALL ANIMALS

Parrot

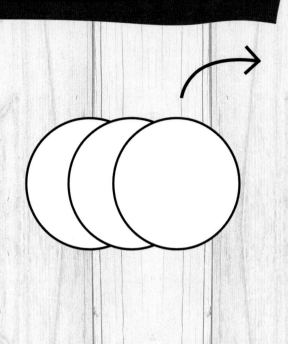

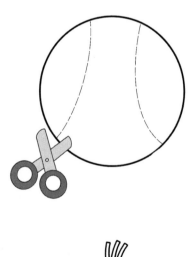

Bat

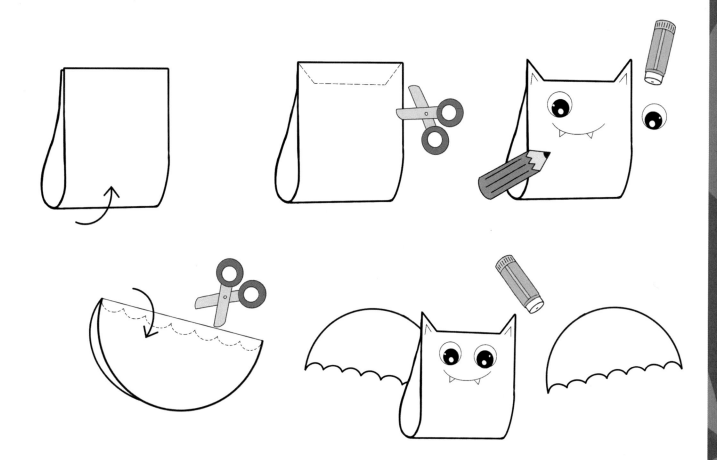

Meerkat

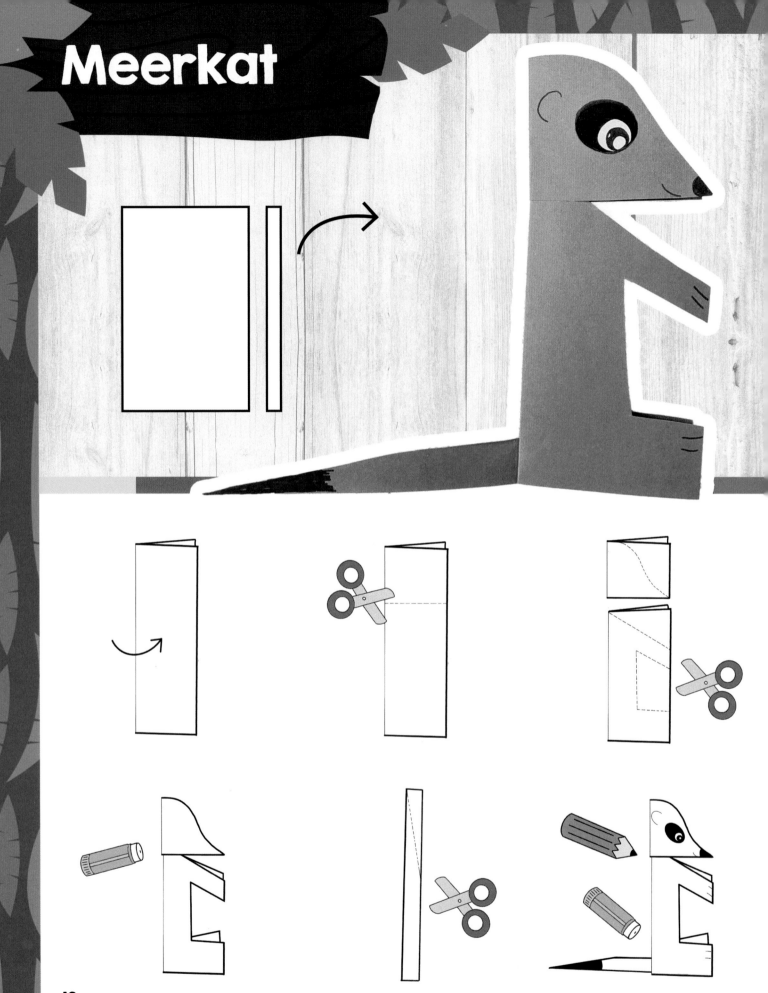

Turtle

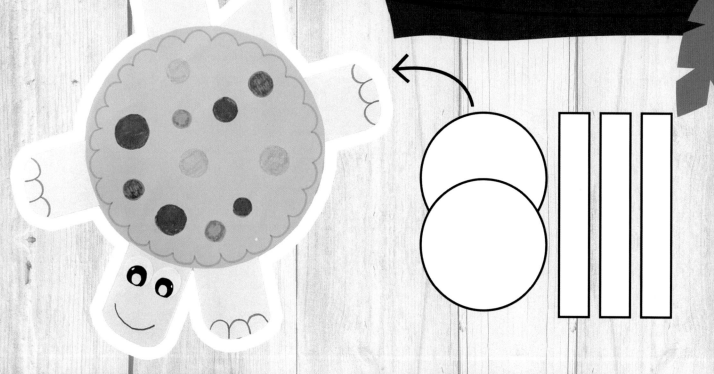

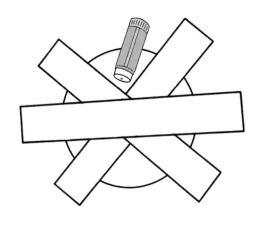

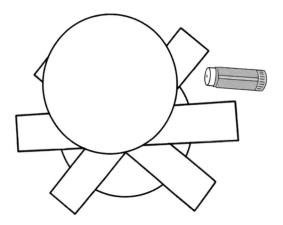

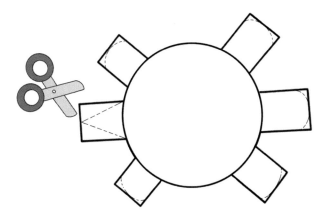

13

Snake

Koala

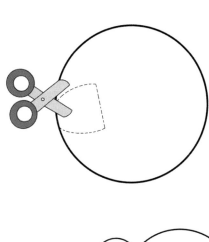

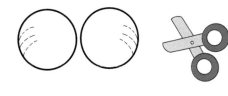

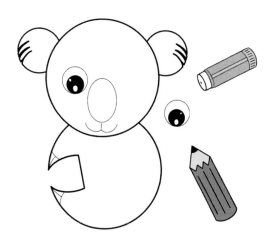

Owl

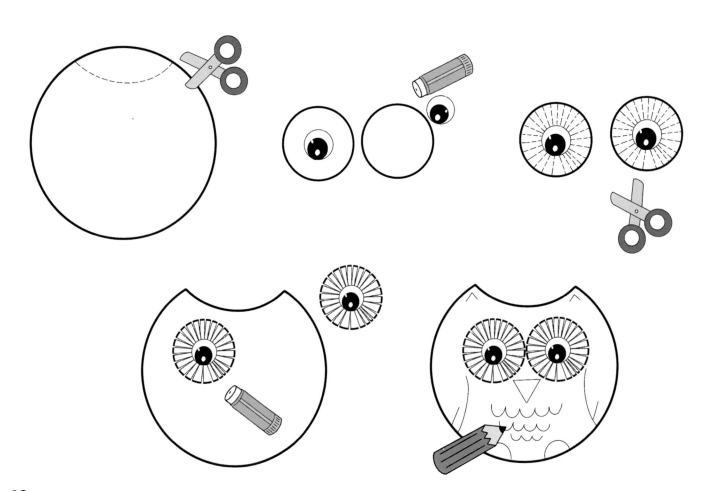

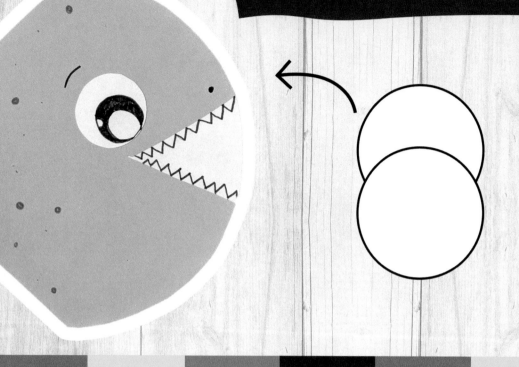

Piranha

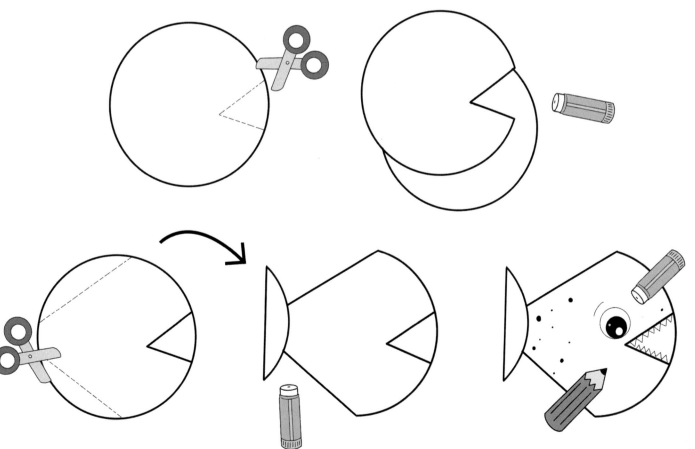

Spider

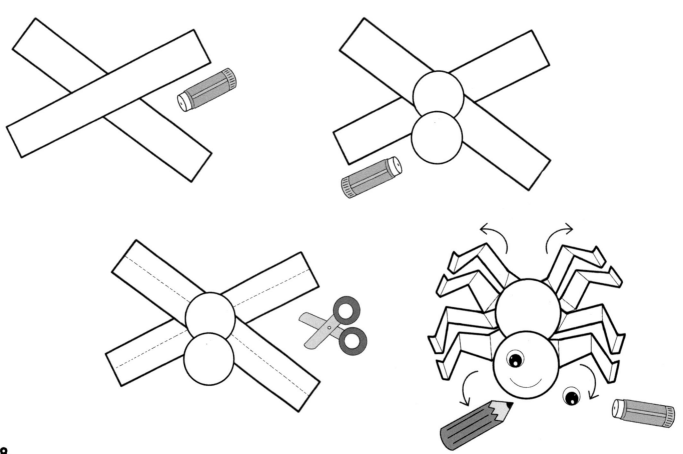

Toucan

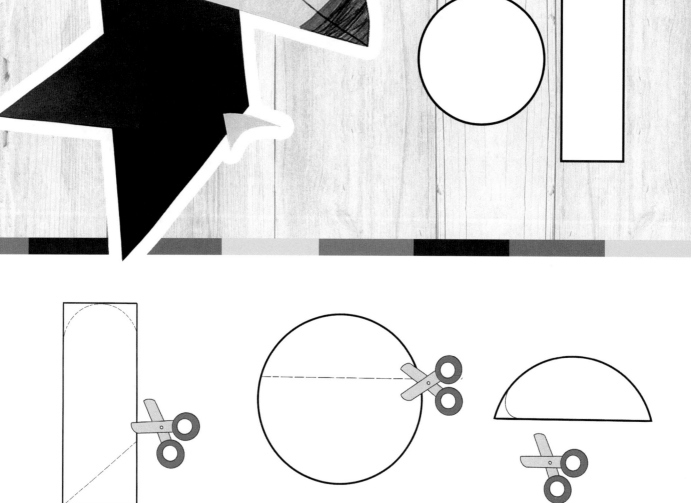

MEDIUM

ANIMALS

Kangaroo

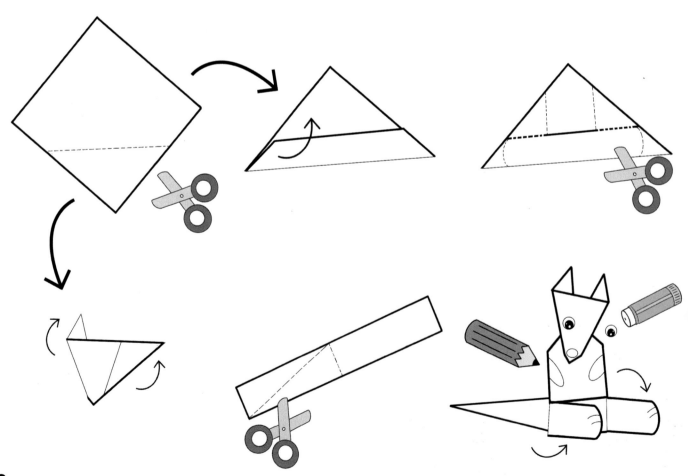

Seal

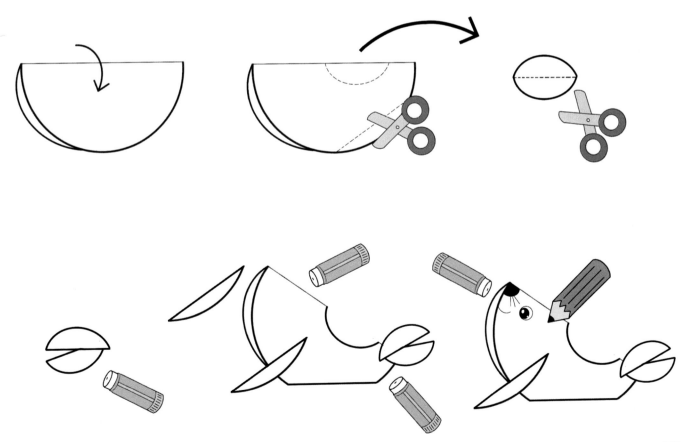

Crocodile

Leopard

Lion

Monkey

27

Peacock

Panda

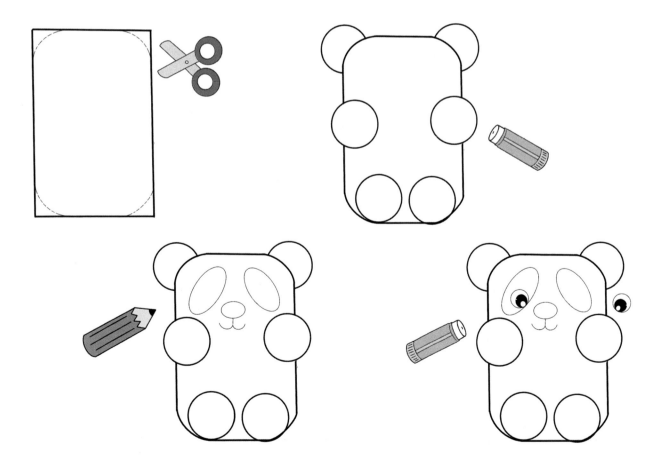

Penguin

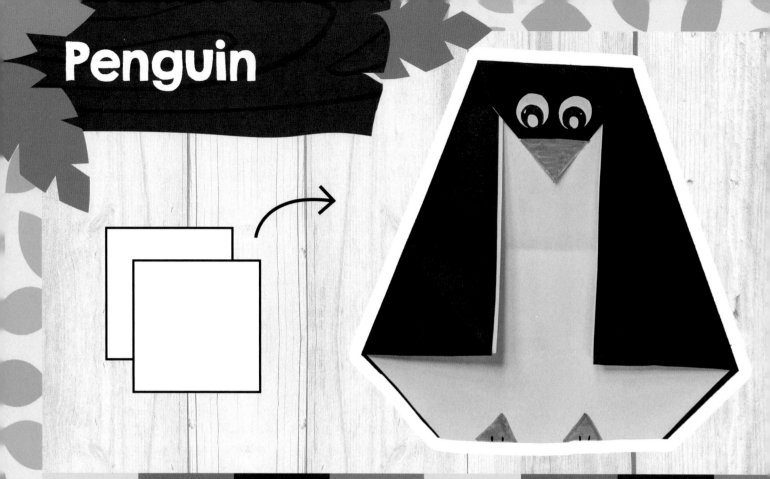

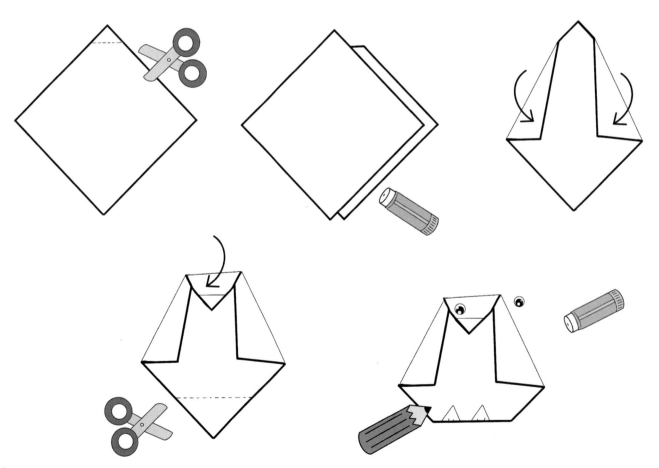

Porcupine

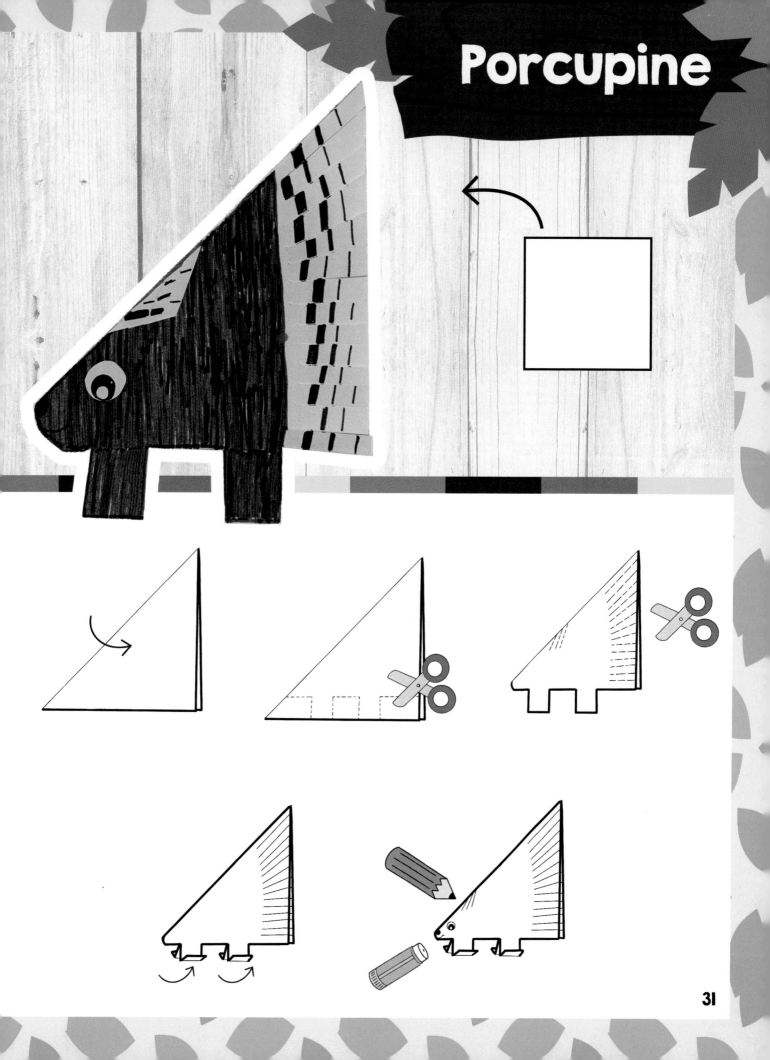

Wolf

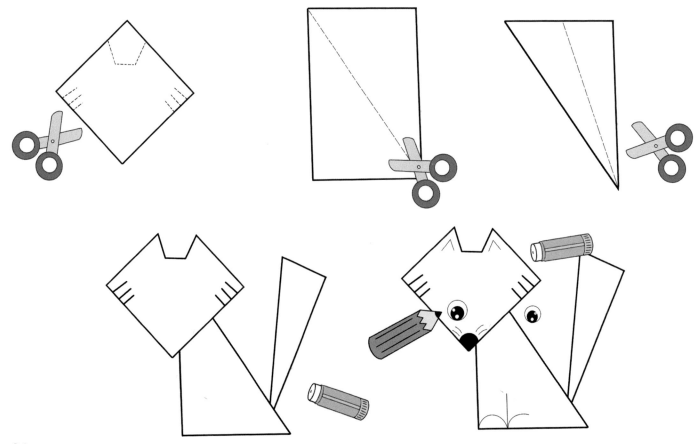

Tiger

33

LARGE ANIMALS

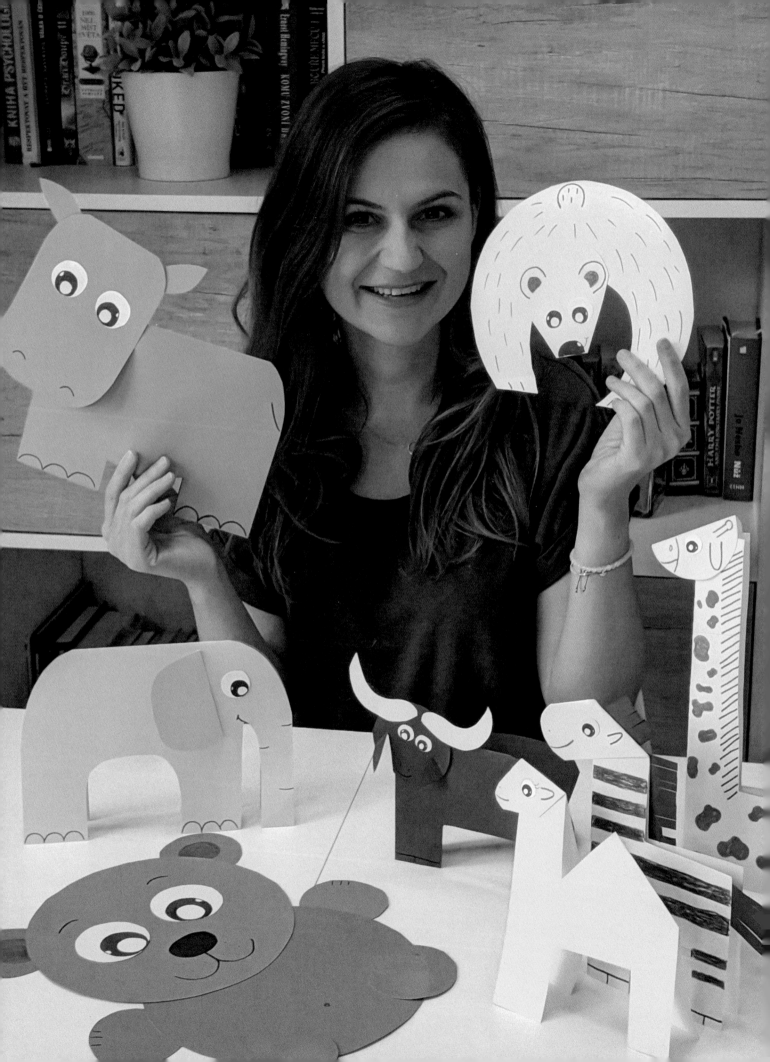

Buffalo

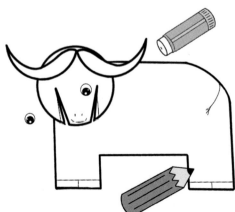

Polar Bear

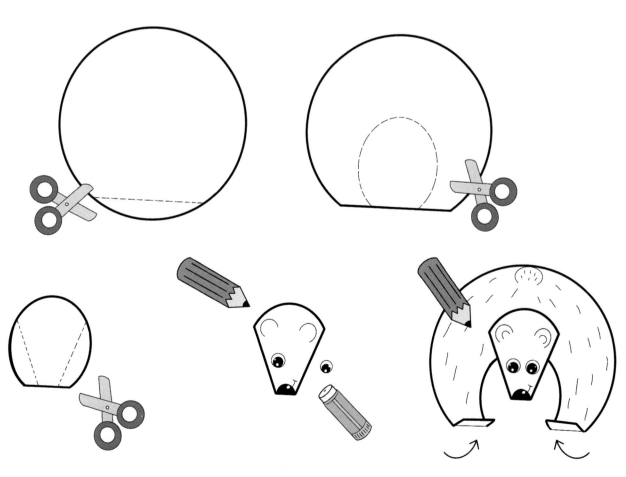

37

Hippo

Giraffe

39

Bear

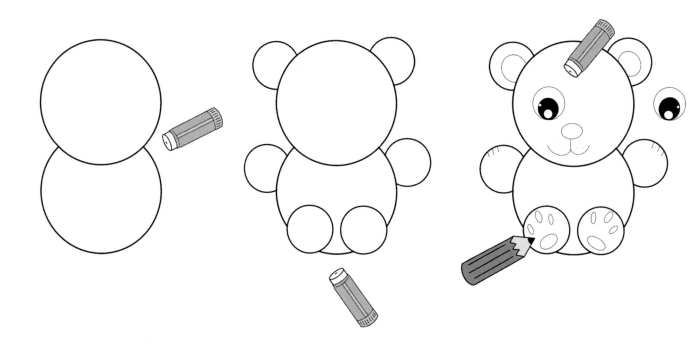

Elephant

Zebra

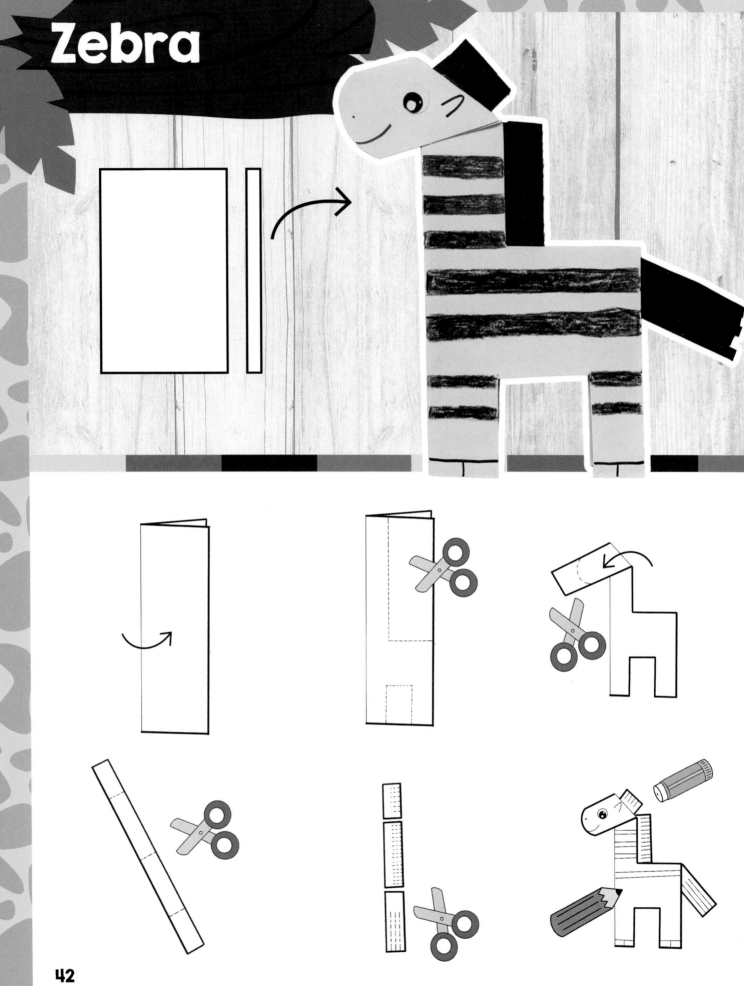

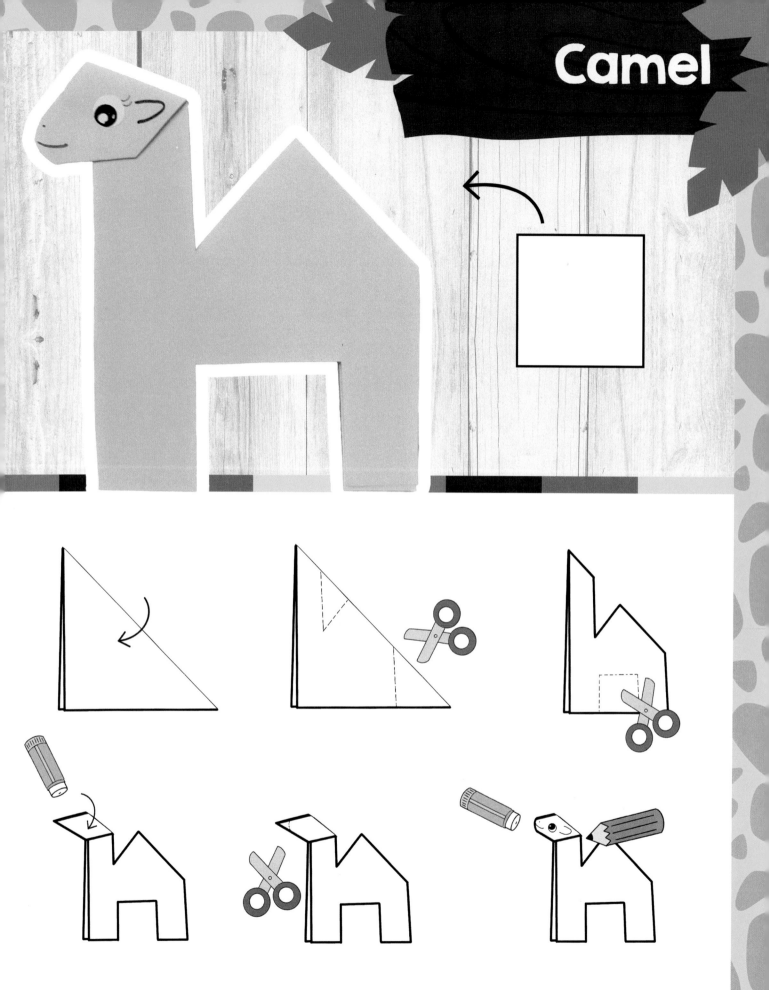

Camel

43